Praise For:

Living Your Greater Life Devotional and Bible Study

The desire for greatness is truly contagious. When you see that attribute being modeled by someone you admire, a spark ignites on the inside of you and if you embrace it, you immediately begin to rise. From the moment I heard Dr. Derrick Love speak on the subject of greatness, my heart began to stir with holy inspiration. He is a motivator, a messenger, and a mentor to those who want to use their gifts for God and people. Without a doubt, he'll inspire you as well.

   —Babbie Mason, Dove Award-winning singer,songwriter, author, and speaker. www.babbie.com

***

Living Your Greater Devotional and Bible Study: A Companion to Your Greater is Right Now is a great supplement to the original book. Having read the initial book, one thing I discovered is the need to have a daily focus on living out the "greater is now" principles. The devotionals are real, relevant, and right on time given the seasons of life we experience while pursuing greatness. The words come to life through scripture and I can hear the encouraging words coming from Dr. Love as he shares what God has given him for this project. Each day is packed with enough spiritual sustenance to sustain you as you journey towards greater in the Kingdom of God!

—**Kenneth M. Chapman Jr., Ph.D**. Associate Pastor, Life Changing Faith Christian Fellowship.

***

As water rises to greater levels as more is added to it, so God created us to be filled with His Word so we, too, may rise to greater levels. In *Living Your Greater Devotional And Bible Stydy: A Companion To Your Greater Is Right Now*, Dr. Derrick Love walks you through the process of self-examination to seal the cracks that make us leak and prevent us from fulfilling our God-given assignments. Knowing who we are and where we spiritually leak brings us into a deeper relationship with God and allows the Potter to patch us up to be Our Greater Now. Imagine the joy and new sense of identity in the Messiah when you grab hold of the biblical truths of what God has to say about you and what He designed you to accomplish for the Kingdom. The only one stopping you from Your Greater is you and now you have the keys to unlock your full Kingdom potential. Dr. Derrick Love guides you on the journey of a lifetime to find our true calling and grow in new and exciting ways.

—**Rabbi Eric Walker,** Executive Director, Igniting a Nation Ministries.

After reading Dr. Derrick Love's new devotional based on his outstanding book, Your Greater Is Right Now, I am impressed with his devotional and Bible study, *Living Your Greater Devotional and Bible Study*. What readers will find in Dr. Love's new book is a blueprint for a focused sixty-day journey to a more fulfilling, more intimate, more powerful walk with God. Dr. Love continues his strong writing style with Bible-based exhortation and winsome admonishment. He reminds readers that our life in Christ is waiting to be fulfilled as we faithfully and obediently travel the road of life, fueled by the promises of God for our victory.

— **Dr. Mike Spaulding,** Pastor of *Calvary Chapel of Lima.* Host, Dr. Mike Live.

LIVING YOUR GREATER LIFE DEVOTIONAL & BIBLE STUDY

A Companion To Your Greater Is Right Now

Dr. Derrick Love

Published by KHARIS PUBLISHING, imprint of
KHARIS MEDIA LLC.

Copyright © 2021 Dr. Derrick Love

ISBN-13: 978-1-63746-067-2

ISBN-10: 1-63746-067-8

Library of Congress Control Number: 2021909785

All Scripture quotations, unless otherwise indicated, are
taken from the Holy Bible, New Revised Standard
Version®, RSV®. Copyright ©1973, 1978, 1984, 2011
by Biblical, Inc.™ Used by permission.

All KHARIS PUBLISHING products are available at
special quantity discounts for bulk purchase for sales
promotions, premiums, fund-raising, and educational
needs. For details, contact:

Kharis Media LLC
Tel: 1-479-599-8657
support@kharispublishing.com
www.kharispublishing.com

TABLE OF CONTENTS

DAY 1

GREATNESS IS YOUR HERITAGE

"Greater is he that is in you, than he that is in the world."

1 John 4:4 (KJV)

Whether you're a single mom or family man, you're in business or you're working for someone, one thing is certain: you have your picture of greatness. Somewhere, somehow, you've got a model for greatness, and you're always chasing after it. You want to constantly look like that picture you've got in your mind!

But alas! Can I tell you something today? Everyone has equal potential to be great! What do I mean? Greatness is not limited to some set of people, neither is it removed from the path of others. Greatness is not synonymous with culture, tribe, race, or nationality. Greatness is defined as an individual's inner will to achieve success and their capacity to increase exponentially in faith.

In a play titled "Twelfth Night," the playwright William Shakespeare wrote, *"Some are born great, some achieve greatness, and some have greatness thrust upon them."* What is he pointing out? Everyone has the potential to be great. Yes, including you! In our bible verse today; we saw that the one you have within you is the determinant of how great you are or will become. In fact, it says, the seed inside you is greater than the world put together.

Key Success Tip 1:

Choose joy today
because He lives in you.

REFLECTION

Do you perceive yourself to be small and insignificant whenever you see great minds and influencers in your field? The truth is, *"You were designed for accomplishment, engineered for success, and endowed with the seeds of greatness."* –Zig Ziglar.

ACTION POINT

Write two words to reengage your mind.

_____

_____

Will you start thinking and taking steps that make for greatness? Identify two-steps today that you will begin to implement.

_____

_____

_____

_____

_____

DAY 2

IGNORE UNPREDICTABLE TIMELINES

"Though the mountains be shaken and the hills be removed, yet my unfailing love for you will not be shaken, nor my covenant of peace be removed, says the lord, who has compassion on you."

Isaiah 54:10 (NIV)

The indisputable truth is that at some point in life, we go through seasons when we aren't sure what's up next. Life will present us with hardships and unpredictable timelines. Now, if these happen with no disruptions in our everyday life, it would have been tolerable for many. But, these unpredictable timelines tend to devalue our faith and confidence in humanity, nature, and even God.

For instance, the world is facing a global pandemic called COVID-19 right now, an unsettling virus impacting on nations, countries, and institutions. Every day, mainstream media releases new evidence of the devastating impact of COVID-19 (the invisible lining) across the world. The statistics of infected persons and those who have died from the pandemic have only compounded fear and despair among men and women.

> ## Key Success Tip 2:
>
> Dig Deep today to unpack your worth.

REFLECTION

Amid these uncertain times, you may question your faith? Or despise God's promises? Are you still rooted in Him? Remember that nothing should shake you, *"...for he hath said, I will never leave thee, nor forsake thee."* (Hebrews 13:5; Deuteronomy 31:6).

ACTION POINT

What are your greatest fears and concerns today?

_____

_____

What are the thoughts that you will no longer allow to shake your faith in God? Be Specific.

_____

_____

_____

_____

_____

_____

DAY 3

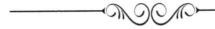

YOU CAN SPROUT AGAIN!

"Even a tree has more hope! If it is cut down, it will sprout again and grow new branches."

Job 14:7 (NLT)

Sprouting again means the ability to rise above your present state, the circumstances around you, the economy, or unhealthy predictions. It's the unyielding, come-back attitude in you to any situation that comes your way. Many people easily give up at the slightest sense of threat and discomfort. They forget so quickly that the journey to greatness is never without the speed bumps or challenges.

Yes! These speed bumps are never there to stop the flow of life within you, but to help you rest in God and launch out again in newness of strength. So, rather than follow unpredictable timelines and get discouraged with the twist of life, why not trust God to see you through? The bible recounts that the righteous shall fall seven times but always come back stronger and better (Proverbs 24:16, KJV).

Key Success Tip 3:

Remember the promise He's placed within you. No turning back!

REFLECTION

Have setbacks made you give up on your journey to greatness? Emulate the wisdom of King David and say, *"In my distress, I called upon the LORD; to my God, I cried for help. From his temple, he heard my voice, and my cry to him reached his ears"* Psalms 18:6 (ESV).

Tell your fear; I've got a come-back plan—the Lord!

ACTION POINT

What challenges of life have pushed you down in recent times?

_____

_____

What steps have you resolved to take in order to bounce back to the path of greatness?

_____

_____

_____

You need to shake off the disappointments and the failures, and believe you can still succeed as you advance into your greatness.

_____

_____

_____

DAY 4

WHAT IS YOUR MENTAL DESIGN?

"For as he thinks within himself, so is he..."

Proverbs 23:7 (NASB)

Do you see from the scriptural verse above what mirrors a man's greatness and destiny? Yes, it's the mental design. Your mental design is your destiny because it's the depth of what your mind can conceive that you can actualize or become.

Think about this for a moment. Can any building be bigger, better, or more beautiful than its architectural plan and design? For instance, Burj Khalifa, in Dubai, which stands at 829.8m high as the tallest building in the world today, has 163 floors.

Indeed, the citizens of Dubai didn't lazily crawl out of bed one sunny morning to find that massive edifice. No, they didn't! People painstakingly designed it. And it's not possible to have a design for a duplex and expect to construct a skyscraper.

> ## Key Success Tip 4:
>
> You are a "Masterpiece" designed for greatness.

REFLECTION

What model do you have in your mind for your life? What tools are you using for the plans in your life? Are you shooting for greatness or mediocrity?

ACTION POINT

What is your most dominant thought? Is it greatness or mediocrity?

_____

_____

Take the bull by the horn and paint a great design of a glorious destiny on the canvas of your mind!

_____

_____

Dream big and think great today.

_____

_____

_____

DAY 5

RESET YOUR PRIORITIES

"There is a time for everything, a season for every activity under heaven."

Ecclesiastes 3:1 (NLT)

Activities seem to be the human default mode, and we always want to be productive. Naturally, when you are idle, you feel wasted and undone. Certainly, it's an unpleasant feeling, especially when you have many plans to execute, many thoughts to process, and they all seem tangled. The super power everyone wishes for in such situations is the ability to prioritize perfectly.

You might have experienced this kind of phase before now. That's an indication you need to reset your priorities. Talking about priority, for many years, I thought fulfillment was about how much I fit into the interest and expectations of others. I failed to invest in myself and what will make me of greater value to others.

Sincerely, you can't afford to miss the process of investing in yourself as you target greatness. There are behaviors you need to improve on - learning to undertake, plans to draft on your future, and more— you need growth generally. It's high time you reset your priorities.

Indeed, there's a need to place your interests rightly so that you can embark on a seamless run of productivity. Interests vary among humans, and it will be gainful to map out what constitutes your preference as a Christian. As Jesus said, *"For which of you, intending to build a tower, sitteth not down first, and counteth the cost, whether he have sufficient to finish it?"* (Luke 14:28 KJV)

> # Key Success Tip 5:
>
> Be intentional today.
> Rely on God to move it.

REFLECTION

Do you desire a great life? Are you willing to be of value to others by implementing a reset in your priorities? To be responsible, you must be decisive and productive. Disorganized ideas will pose a threat to your goal. Are you inspired and ready to push the reset button?

ACTION POINT

Make a list of your daily routine and arrange them in order of priority.

_____

_____

What activities or engagements do you invest your time in that tends not to add value to you?

_____

_____

Make a list of two things you will invest in yourself today that will lead to your greatness.

_____

_____

_____

_____

DAY 6

DISCOVER YOUR PURPOSE

"For we are God's masterpiece. He has created us anew in Christ Jesus, so that we can do the good things he planned for us long ago."

Ephesians 2:10 (NLT)

Are you wondering what I mean? I mean discovering what you are to contribute to humanity and investing every sweat that graces your brow to produce your foreordained greatness.

Ask yourself these big questions: "Why am I here?" "What am I born to do?" "Am I relevant to my world?" The answers to your inquiry lie in your ability to understand and utilize your nature and design. Until you come to a point where you know the purpose of your existence, you'll continue to struggle with reality. Imagine square pegs trying to fit in round holes. Talk about an epic fail!

You have been equipped for the purpose for which you were called, this is inherent in you, and you played practically no part in this equipping process (John 15:16). Knowing this, "To whom much is given, much is expected." Jesus rebuked the servant that buried his talent of gold because he made no profitable stewardship of the lot he was to manage. Matthew 25:18 says, *"But the servant who received the one bag of silver dug a hole in the ground and hid the master's money for safe keeping."*

Key Success Tip 6:

Rediscover "you" today
in the image of Christ.

REFLECTION

Have you found your purpose? What are your contributions to humanity? Are you doing the will of the Lord at the moment? *"But the master replied, "You wicked and lazy servant! You think I'm a hard man, do you? Harvesting crops I didn't plant and gathering crops I didn't cultivate? Well, you should at least have put my money into the bank so I could have some interest."* (Mathew 25:26-27)

ACTION POINT

It's time to take conscious steps to find out why you are here on earth.

_____

_____

Have you discovered your purpose? Invest in it and stay where you belong.

_____

_____

DAY 7

THINK INTENTIONALLY

"And now, dear brothers and sisters, let me say one more thing as I close this letter. Fix your thoughts on what is true and honorable and right. Think about things that are pure and lovely and admirable. Think about things that are excellent and worthy of praise."

Philippians 4:8 (NLT)

Self-sabotaging thoughts and self-limiting confessions are self-directed arrows. Usually, it is your mindset that starts losing the battles, then it becomes executed through the mouth. Your mouth is the gateway to your realities; what you say and think about ends up molding your realities in life, whether good or otherwise.

One way you can achieve greatness is to guard your heart with all diligence; it is written, *"Above all else, guard your heart, for it affects everything you do. Avoid all perverse talk; stay far from corrupt speech"* (Proverbs 4: 23-24 NLT).

Thoughts are crucial; from your thoughts, you can identify a life governed by the divine spirit from the fleshly nature. *"Those who are dominated by the sinful nature think about sinful things, but those who are controlled by the Holy Spirit think about things that please the spirit"* (Romans 8:5 NLT).

Key Success Tip 7:

Be relentless in your pursuit for purpose.

REFLECTION

What are your thoughts? Your thoughts should always allow the Holy Spirit to have HIS way. Is your heart pure? "God blesses those whose hearts are pure, for they will see God (Mathew 5:8 NLT)."

ACTION POINT

How high can you see yourself rise on the ladder of greatness?

_____

_____

Don't allow any self-limiting thought to settle in your mind.

_____

_____

Think only of the promises of God, which are YES and AMEN and avoid obvious challenges.

_____

_____

Unlocking Your Greater

As you conclude this week, what were some of your greatest challenges and successes? And, what are the next steps to continue your forward movement into this upcoming week?

_____

_____

_____

_____

_____

_____

_____

_____

_____

_____

_____

_____

_____

_____

_____

_____

"You Are A Masterpiece"

DAY 8

HARNESS YOUR POTENTIAL

"Do you see any truly competent workers? They will serve kings rather than ordinary people."

Proverbs 22:29 (NLT)

Many people are held back by limiting beliefs and fears that have prevented them from fully harnessing the gifts that God has placed in them. These destructive energies have produced negative self-worth.

For instance, no matter the potential in a seed, it will dry up from the root when it is not nurtured. Steady watering and pruning are necessary for the germination of a seed to fruiting. This is the same manner you must nurture the seed of greatness in you.

Never contemplate fear as you aim to get better, be spirited regardless of the seeming obstacles. A bestselling author once said, *"Talent is never enough without the input of hard work."*

Endeavor to keep productive friends who are of like passion, detest laziness, and don't take *"no"* for an answer; remember that iron sharpens iron.

Subject yourself to reading informative and encouraging words. Speak with authority regarding your greatness. Depend heavily on the Lord's assurances as you exercise faith.

Key Success Tip 8:

Choose to believe today despite what it looks like or feels.

REFLECTION

Does the stranglehold of fear becloud your potential? Christ says, "fear not, for I'll be with you always." How will you reach your potential if you hold on to beliefs that limit you? The word of God is strong enough to tear down all strongholds!

ACTION POINT

Have you discovered your God-given potential?

_____

_____

It's time to nurture and guard it till it grows and bears fruit for all humanity.

_____

_____

Make a list of your five closest friends. Is your friendship helping you advance to your greatness or quenching your zeal for greatness?

_____

_____

DAY 9

INVEST IN YOURSELF

"You shall eat the fruit of the labor of your hands; you shall be blessed, and it shall be well with you."

Psalm 128:2 (ESV)

Have you ever taken yourself out on a treat to celebrate a worthy achievement? I want you to know that you deserved it. Often, beyond a "thumbs up" luxury and a sensational experience of pleasure, there is a need to connect with yourself on a deeper level. Just as when you invest your money in foreign or local trade, you need to weigh your life's potential to know if it is a loss or gain.

Know that you'll get what you give, whether to others or yourself. Find out your strengths and accentuate them, discover your weaknesses, and work on them. Expose yourself to **GREATER** ideas and dedicate time for persistent pursuit. Grab a hold of your dreams and capitalize on the necessary sacrifice and training needed to become your best version. Connect with your core—your essence as a human being—and dedicate your life to being who you truly are as you accomplish extraordinary rewards. Your future deserves greater.

Key Success Tip 9:

What you invest in is what you will get out of it. You are worth the investment!

REFLECTION

Think about this; you are accountable only to yourself and not anyone. If you fall short of the fullness of your purpose, do you think anyone is to blame? You have all it takes already.

ACTION POINT

Here are some ways you can invest in your spirit, soul, and body:

- Pray, meditate, and study God's Word daily.

- Create a vision board of your goals.

- Create a daily or weekly check-inform to monitor your progress.

- Journal your thoughts daily or weekly to keep yourself motivated and engaged toward the goals.

- Celebrate small victories because it's a motivational factor to achieving your long-term goals. What are your small victories today?

_____

_____

_____

_____

DAY 10

GOD'S GRACE IS NOT NEGOTIABLE

"I am what I am by the grace of God."

1 Corinthians 15:10 (KJV)

As we progress along life's forward track, hard work, discipline, and persistence are inevitable. You have to brace up if you must run life's race. But the truth is, our sufferings and personal denials alone can't get us to our destination. We will always need divine intervention.

God's grace is key if we must overcome life's trouble and obtain a crown at the end of our race. Similar to the experience of Apostle Paul, we are constantly aware of what's needful and right to do but may still fall back to engaging in irrelevant, inexpedient activities, which is to one's detriment.

God has not ordained the hit-and-miss life for you. Rather, He wants to help you through your life's journey. He wants to substitute His favor for your labor, His grace for your race, and disgrace. Even as He said to Apostle Paul more than 2000 years ago, he is echoing these burden-lifting, life-transforming words to you, saying: *"My grace is sufficient for you."*

You can't successfully navigate your journey without the grace of God, Neither can you reach your highest peaks without the hand of God's grace ordering your footsteps. Laced with the divine rhythm of grace, our personal and collective efforts will rhyme dutifully into harmonious lines of incredible, supernatural results.

Key Success Tip 10:

Persistence is the key to
success. Keep pushing today!

REFLECTION

You are not ordained to run life's race in your
strength. Your happiness and ultimate fulfillment
stem from God's unmerited help—His grace. Who
is helping you get through life's hurdles; God or
yourself?

ACTION POINT

What aspect of your life are you struggling with to
succeed?

_____

_____

Come to God boldly and obtain grace to help in
achieving greatness with ease.

_____

_____

DAY 11

TAKE OFF YOUR MASKS

"Do not conform to the pattern of this world, but be transformed by the renewing of your mind..."

Romans 12:2 (NIV)

Can you imagine getting used to a pair of glasses that makes you feel empty and incomplete when you don't wear them? A mask can be of same effect, but in this case, a cover-up of the real, inward feelings. Today in the world, several people go about with an emotional façade to substitute die-hard, existent traits. Plastic smiles, fake facial expression: a greater percentage would do anything to fit in and belong within society's context.

But does God want this from or for you? Trying to fit in the world with a fake identity will only do more harm than good. Is God proud that you substitute the truthfulness of your heart for lies and deception? You were made for greatness, and the world does not get to define it for you.

God cares that you approach Him with sincerity of heart. He wants you to be transformed, not by your family, friends, or society's opinion about you, but through the renewal of your mind by His word. Let go of the pretense and, in turn, the weight of pretending.

> # Key Success Tip 11:
>
> Self- reflection is critical for your success. Remove the mask to tap into your greater.

REFLECTION

How well are you doing with all your efforts to fit in? Your seat of greatness is unique; you don't need to fake your way through it.

ACTION POINT

Be willing to fully unmask so that you begin to define or redefine your greatness. Which masks are you currently wearing?

_____

_____

What steps are you willing to take today to remove the masks you are wearing?

_____

_____

DAY 12

DO NOT HIDE YOUR PAIN

*"For we do not have a high priest
who is unable to sympathize with
our weaknesses..."*

Hebrew 4:16 (ESV)

Have you been broken and bruised due to past hurts,
failures, and traumatic experiences? Imagine you
visit a clinic to check a bad toe. You will have to
communicate your pain to the physician before you
get adequate treatment or a piece of medical advice.
Every often, people find it easier to steer attention

away from their pain with the simple phrase, "I'm fine," even during the times when they feel crushed.

Many people don't think it is nice to bother people with their problems, yet every part of their bodies cry for help and rescue. What's worse is that folks extend this attitude to their Creator. Contrarily, God is eager to render help whenever we call. He is not just aware of our pain and distresses; He also gets to feel them. You aren't going through this all by yourself; you've got God to carry you!

Key Success Tip 12:

Replace your past hurt & pain with truth. You are made in the image of Christ.

REFLECTION

It's ok to cry; yes it doesn't make you weak; it only makes you human. But what you do next is what differentiates a star from a mediocre.

ACTION POINT

Talk to God about your troubles and soul-wrenching pains.

_____

_____

You have tried it on your own; it's time to hand it over.

_____

_____

DAY 13

LET IT GO!

"Leave all your worries with him, because he cares for you."

1 Peter 5:7 (GNT)

You can't let go unless you forgive yourself first. Probably, you're hurt and want to take your revenge, and you can't think of how to move on without getting your offender to swallow a dose of their own medicine. Anyway, I can assure you of the promise of a greater life of quality and freedom if you are only willing to forgive.

Rather than being drowned in the sea of unforgiveness, grab on Christ's anchor of pure and genuine love. Allow God's love to work its soothing miracles of healing and grace in you. Cast your struggles, shame, and pain on Him as you let His love flow outwardly from you to others, even your greatest offender.

Unforgiveness is a barricade on your way to greatness. It robs you of rest, joy, and peace of mind. Rather than hiding behind the mask to please others and remain hurt, unmask yourself and embrace the wholeness in Jesus.

Key Success Tip 13:

You are a gift from God and you are perfect in His sight. Give yourself a hug.

REFLECTION

God's plan for you has no limit to greatness, but how high can an eagle soar when her wing is pegged to a tree? Don't place the limit on your life; let it go!

ACTION POINT

Today, make a personal commitment to consciously and deliberately take off the mask right now—the mask that has veiled you from the beauty and reality of life.

_____

_____

It's time to call that man or that lady you are holding a grudge against and forgive them from your heart so you can enjoy the fullness of the finished work of Christ.

_____

_____

DAY 14

NEVER SETTLE FOR LESS

"For I know the plans I have for you, declares the Lord, plans for welfare and not for evil, to give you a future and a hope."

Jeremiah 29:11 (ESV)

Anyone can meticulously plan, anybody can experience a flurry of winning steaks, but not everyone can adequately settle. Our world wants our past moments in life to define and determine success, but sadly, believers are inclined to accept these standards as true.

Most times, we fight to the tooth to attain the contemporary specifications of what success is, at the expense of what God says it really is. Truly, no matter how sophisticated or charming the picture of accomplishment, achievements, and fulfillment has been painted in society's fabric, we have a better heritage with Christ.

Candidly, our reality in Christ is the ultimate and should be what we settle for. Who has God called you to be? What divine purpose or assignment is required from you? This is what you should aim to represent. Whether you feel like you measure up to the world's standard or not, God sees you as the best person for what He called you to do. So, keep fighting and keep expecting greater!

Key Success Tip 14:

Remove the limits and barriers of your past, present, and future. You are already a winner!

REFLECTION

When you are at the center of God's plan for your life, you should depend on God to get you to your destination. Whatever is not in His word for you is not your worth.

ACTION POINT

What have you accepted as your standard and specification of greatness?

_____

_____

It's time to settle with God's word and discover what God is thinking about you and what He has designed for you in His master plan.

_____

_____

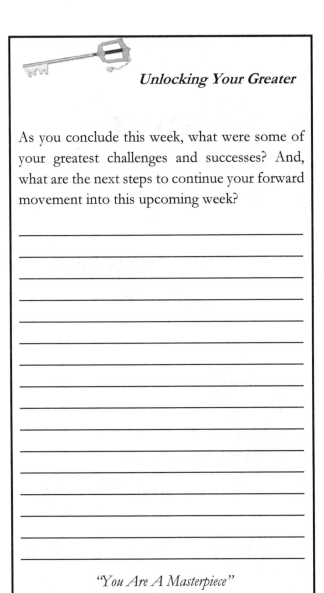

Unlocking Your Greater

As you conclude this week, what were some of your greatest challenges and successes? And, what are the next steps to continue your forward movement into this upcoming week?

_____

_____

_____

_____

_____

_____

_____

_____

_____

_____

_____

_____

_____

_____

_____

"You Are A Masterpiece"

DAY 15

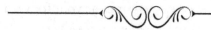

DISCOVER YOUR TRUE IDENTITY

"Before I formed you in the womb I knew you, before you were born I set you apart; I appointed you as a prophet to the nations."

Jeremiah 1:5 (NIV)

A life with the right identity is one that showcases a picture of the right perspective. The media, our parents, and even our environment grapple with feeding us with stereotyped ideas of who we are and who we ought to be. However, neither of these holds the true definition of our identity, and following their strategies would only lead us off our original designs.

The quality of your life is proportional to the sense of your identity. And, until you see yourself in the right light, your life will be patterned erroneously. Man's true identity is unveiled by His Creator, His manufacturer, and no one else. Seeing yourself from God's view is the perfect and most wholesome outlook. It guarantees a firm, lasting foundation that will withstand and outlast the most challenging situations.

Also, the moment you discover your identity, your life begins to shift in the right direction. Like a dream of the night, things start to fall into place. Everything begins to work in your favor, and you can trust God to see you through what you do not understand. A heart-rooted in conviction and a verbal declaration about who you are in Christ is the anchor in the storm.

Key Success Tip 15:

You are enough! Take yourself on a date with purpose today.

REFLECTION

I am what God says I am. Meditate on this: *"Although you have been forsaken and hated, with no one traveling through, I will make you the everlasting pride and the joy of all generations"* (Isaiah 60:15).

ACTION POINT

To find your true identity, identify with the word of God and who He says you are.

_____

_____

Have a defined time and place to meditate on God's word so it can correct the defect in your life.

_____

_____

DAY 16

GOD HAS THE PERFECT LENS

"This means that anyone who belongs to Christ has become a new person. The old life is gone; a new life has begun!"

2 Corinthians 5:17 (NIV)

Those who wear old lens might fall into the dissatisfying habit of changing their spectacles only when there is a crack or breakage. Even in greater matters, many individuals unconsciously assume the habit of viewing life from popular opinions of people who lived before them, findings and research of philosophers or scientists, etc.

In any case, there is a new way, a new perspective to see things. The Bible teaches in 2 Corinthians 5:17 that *"...anyone who belongs to Christ has become a new person. The old life is gone; a new life begins!"* As a believer, you should not let the conclusions of others determine your course in life. You should not subject your life to men's expectation, but you should put all your trust in God for He cares for you.

God holds the perfect lens to discovering your true identity—your actual reality. Which clarifying or magnifying lens you use doesn't matter because God has the vision of the right lens. And if you care, of course, you do care about seeing yourself in the right light; you opt for the lens that God only holds to see your glorious and bright future seamlessly.

Key Success Tip 16:

Do not be afraid to launch into the deep today!

REFLECTION

What do you see of yourself in a few years? Your greatness and success must be real to you before it becomes a reality.

ACTION POINT

Desire to see your life through God's brand-new impeccable lens of His word.

_____

_____

DAY 17

APPEAL TO PRAYER

"And call upon me in the day of trouble: I will deliver thee, and thou shalt glorify me".

Psalm 50:15 (KJV)

Often, life's journey takes us through turbulent shark-infested waters. Our boat gets rocked violently, and the troubled sea threatens to tip our vessels and leave us helpless in the perilous waters. In times like this, we need an anchor, something to stabilize us and help us survive. Indeed, when they're impossibilities all around, it's time to pave the way through prayer.

So, what lets you into a place of no limitations when all you can see is hopelessness? The answer is prayer! *Prayer* is the gatekeeper to attract God's attention toward your situation or circumstance. It connects you with God's heart for your journey.

No matter what you're going through, praying to your Father is the way to get right back on course. You might think you're out of reach and no one can get you out of the deep waters you're in, but immediately you call on God, you'll appear on the radar again. Right then, you'll begin to hear God's precious whispers that help to direct your steps. However, God wants to hear you open up in away that is authentic and genuine.

In times of trouble, all God requires from you is to call on Him in your vulnerability. He says, *"Here I am! I stand at the door and knock. If you hear my voice and open the door, I will come in and eat with you. And you will eat with me."* (Revelations 3:20 ERV).

Key Success Tip 17:

Seek God's direction today as you pursue purpose, passion, and peace through prayer.

REFLECTION

What's your first response to challenging situations? At your weakest moments, do you pave the way with prayer? Jesus called on God in His moments of weakness, *"And there appeared an angel unto him from heaven, strengthening him,"* (Luke 22:43 KJV).

ACTION POINT

Do you have a defined time to communicate with God?

_____

_____

It's time to stop praying by impulse and be deliberate about your prayer time.

_____

_____

DAY 18

STRENGTH FROM PRAYER

"Come now, and let us reason together, saith the LORD."

Isaiah 1:18 (KJV)

Have you been in a situation where it seems like fear and defeat have choked your hopes? That moment when all your strength are gone and even your best shot at greatness is like water flowing down the drain.

Today, I want to give you a foundational principle to launch you into a realm of no limitations. Prayer is the gatekeeper to attract God's attention toward your situation or circumstance. Too often, we are quick to tell people about our problems than we tell God. At other times, we think our situation is too trivial for God to pick an interest. But from the scripture for today, God says come and let's have a chit-chat concerning your issues.

Indeed extraordinary things happen when we pray. We learn from the scriptures an interesting experience when Jesus was too weak to advance into his destiny. However, by the power of prayer, the Bible says in Luke 22:43 KJV, *"And there appeared an angel unto him from heaven, strengthening him."* So we see that we can receive divine strength when we pray, also the change you desire is possible by the power of prayer.

Key Success Tip 18:

Release fear and embrace your true power through prayer.

REFLECTION

Do you have issues that have defied solutions? Why not take advantage of this new day and talk to God about them. Engage the power of fervent and effectual prayer to regain strength, passion, and solution.

ACTION POINT

Sincerely list out your struggles and weaknesses.

_____

_____

Talk to your Heavenly Father about each point in your list and pray by faith.

_____

_____

_____

_____

DAY 19

STORMS ONLY TEST YOUR FAITH

"Verily I say unto you, Whosoever shall say unto this mountain, Be thou taken up and cast into the sea; and shall not doubt in his heart, but shall believe that what he saith cometh to pass; he shall have it."

Mark 11:23 (ASV)

Our life's landscape is filled with valleys and hills, and the terrain sometimes appears impossible to navigate. I mean, are you in a situation that you can't seem to call it anything but "failure." I'm not referring to someday-to-day inconveniences like heavy traffic, a flat tire, or even a hassle at work. I mean difficulties such as an illness or even the death of a loved one. Circumstances that cause you to question the very true essence of God's goodness. Times when your wheel is clogged, and you wonder if God is asleep.

The truth is, as a child of God, storms do not come to sink your faith but to strengthen it and keep you rooted or planted in God. Like Job, God desires that you look sternly at the mountain and send it off. Jesus didn't have a discussion with the storm in Mark 4:39; rather, he simply rebuked it. Therefore, fix your gaze on your greater and like an eagle, spread out your wing in majesty, and soar into victory.

Key Success Tip 19:

Trust the process and allow God to walk with you.

REFLECTION

Have you ever faced rejection, even by the least likely? Or is there a storm around you that makes you question your faith in God?

ACTION POINT

It's time to declare strength in God to secure victory despite the storm through your faith.

_____

_____

This morning, speak solution and greatness, boldly cast out every barrier to your greatness in the name of Jesus.

_____

_____

_____

_____

DAY 20

VISUALIZE THE EXPANSE

"I am giving all this land, as far as you can see, to you and your descendants as a permanent possession."

Genesis 13:15 (NLT)

Vision is the roadmap to achieving **your greatness**. Imagine driving at night with a poor headlamp on the road without a street light. You will agree with me that obeying the speed limit becomes easy. Why? A clear vision enhances your speed to **your greater**.

However, your vision must be conceptualized in your mind and written as well because there is an active response to move when you see it written down. What more, vision defines the limits of your possibilities. It's hard to actualize what you can't envision.

For instance, God had told Abraham several promises concerning his greatness, yet he needed to register the image in his mind. And in the process, God was also training him to focus on big thoughts. You see, as you plan to change your future, do not focus on things or people smaller than what you are hoping for because your focus will either feed your faith or confirm Your fears.

Key Success Tip 20:

The vision before you is the blueprint to greatness.

REFLECTION

What is your focus, and how real is your greatness to you? Have you started taking steps to achieve it? If not, start today, and in no time, you will see the fulfillment of the vision.

ACTION POINT

Your future is great, so focus on great things like Abraham.

_____

_____

Begin to see the reality of your greater even from your minor to move to your greater status today.

_____

_____

DAY 21

MEDITATE ON GOD'S WORD

"This book of the law shall not depart out of thy mouth; but thou shalt meditate therein day and night..."

Joshua 1:8(KJV)

The word of God is our compass in the journey of life. From today's text, Joshua has just taken the leadership of the Israelites after the death of Moses, and God's charge to him, if he must succeed, was to meditate on His word daily.

With today's text, you will fully agree that your inheritance of greatness is in the word of God. Paul said in Act 20:32 KJV, *"And now, brethren, I commend you to God, and to the word of his grace, which is able to build you up, and to give you an inheritance among all them which are sanctified."* So, you need to know what has been freely given to you is the moment for you to seize the opportunity to fulfill His will and purpose for your life.

Although it is a general phenomenon that "seeing is believing", are you still in doubt of the reality of your greatness? Make it a routine to always take time out to meditate on God's word to find out what has been written concerning you. Your discovery will further strengthen your faith and also move God to fulfill His promises.

Key Success Tip 21:

Go into a quiet place or space and allow God to speak to you today.

REFLECTION

What you look at determines the reflection in your life. God is always speaking and He desires that you tune to His frequency.

ACTION POINT

How often do you study the word of God, and for what purpose?

_____

_____

To make the word of God your lifestyle simply means obedience to the word of God. How will you pursue obedience today?

_____

_____

_____

_____

Unlocking Your Greater

As you conclude this week, what were some of your greatest challenges and successes? And, what are the next steps to continue your forward movement into this upcoming week?

_____

_____

_____

_____

_____

_____

_____

_____

_____

_____

_____

_____

_____

_____

"You Are A Masterpiece"

DAY 22

FORTIFY YOUR MIND

"Above all, be careful what you think because your thoughts control your life."

Proverbs 4:23 (ERV)

Have you heard the saying that: "Thoughts are boomerangs, returning with precision to their source?" Our lives usually move in the direction of our dominant thoughts. That is why it's vital to choose your thoughts wisely. Your mind is the seat of possible or impossible actions.

From the bible text today, I want to admonish you to guard your mind and thoughts carefully. An interesting event was recorded in Genesis 11. The people wanted to achieve an unimaginable feat by building a stricture to heaven, and in verse 6, God testified about them and said, *"...and now nothing will be restrained from them, which they have imagined to do."* (KJV). Awesome. What have you also imagined to do?

Greatness begins from the mind. Stephen Richards once said, *"Reality is a projection of your thoughts or the things you habitually think about."* So, it's time to program your mind for success only. Think only about your greatness. Deliberately fortify your mind against negative and self-limiting thoughts, and picture your big dream and the reality of **your greater** even from now.

Key Success Tip 22:

Your words and thoughts have power. Speak positively!

REFLECTION

Whatever thing is good, lovely, pure, full of hope and greatness, such should be the template of your thoughts.

ACTION POINT

What do you fill your mind with?

_____

_____

You need to fill your subconscious mind with the great ideas and possibilities that God has placed in your heart.

_____

_____

_____

_____

DAY 23

LET GOD BE YOUR ANCHOR

"That by two immutable things, in which it was impossible for God to lie, we might have a strong consolation, who have fled for refuge to lay hold upon the hope set before us: Which hope we have as an anchor of the soul, both sure and steadfast..."

Hebrew 6:18-19 (KJV)

You may not appreciate the worth of an anchor until you feel the stress of the storm. The anchor is the holding block that holds the boat in position when the storm arises. No doubt, a storm is part of the human journey. We experience unpleasant moments that seek to toss our faith away from the promises of God for our lives.

Friend, God is the anchor of everything He created. He sustains all things. And that includes your life! What we all withstand in life is determined by the strength of our anchor. What's the foundation of your life? What is the source of your hope?

Today I admonish you to unplug your hope from your money or your connections and anchor your life in God. And when the storms of life arise, you will remain stable and firm in Him.

Key Success Tip 23:

Do not allow the storm to distract you from purpose.

REFLECTION

The storm is not considerate; its goal is to dismantle and carry anything on its path. Are you appropriately fitted in Jesus against the storm?

ACTION POINT

What do you put your hope and trust in?

_____

_____

Is it in God or the temporal factors of life? It's time to direct your heart and the source of your expectation out of the storm of life.

_____

_____

_____

_____

DAY 24

DO YOU MAGNIFY YOUR MOUNTAIN?

"You are tempted in the same way that everyone else is tempted. But God can be trusted not to let you be tempted too much, and he will show you how to escape from your temptations."

1 Corinthians 10:13 (CEV)

The size of an object depends on the lens through which it is viewed. And when we look at any situation through a lens distorted with fear, we begin to magnify every circumstance through those tainted lens. Too often, we allow fear to customize our situation, and before long, we start to see ourselves as the only one currently facing a particular challenge. We let the word of discouragement find footing in our hearts instead of plugging into God's Word for relief.

Such fear drives us away from the pursuit of our greatness. Moses sent twelve spies to check out the land God promised Israel. But ten of them returned with an exaggerated report saying, *"And there we saw the giants, the sons of Anak, which come of the giants: and we were in our own sight as grasshoppers, and so we were in their sight."* (Numbers 13:33 (KJV)). They blew their challenge out of proportion.

Despite your present circumstance, always strive to plug into God. Your situation is not new to Him; He has helped others to navigate their way up in the past. Therefore, He is more than willing to help you also.

Key Success Tip 24:

The vision is greater than circumstance. Stay focused!

REFLECTION

Have you faced such an impossible challenge, and you wonder if you are about to set a record with it? Well, God is saying, come to me, that impossible mountain is my expertise. Will you plug in today?

ACTION POINT

Fix your gaze on God and His word so that you can see you through any challenges that come your way big or small.

_____

_____

_____

Spend time in His presence and let your mind of greatness be in Him.

_____

_____

_____

DAY 25

TAKE OFF THE LIMITS

"I can do all things through Christ which strengtheneth me."

Philippians 4:13 (KJV)

An eagle grew up in a chicken yard and always flap her wings and scratch the ground like the other chickens. One day, a strong wind blew, and the chickens ran for cover under the shade. However, this eagle realized that she could spread her wings comfortably even in the storm. In an attempt to enjoy the wind, she looked up and saw a big eagle soaring in majesty with the storm.

Just then, she gently spread her wings, and that was her last day in the chicken yard. You see, everyone that ever arrived at their greatness will tell you they had to deal with self-limiting thoughts at some point in their journey. The thought your not good enough or you are not up to the task.

The scripture for today points that you can do just anything by leaning on the strength of Christ, just like the eagle trusted the strength of the wind. Take the limits off, lift your head, and soar high above mediocrity. You have a place at the top.

Key Success Tip 25:

There is no greater joy when you fully realize there are no limits in Christ.

REFLECTION

What stops others cannot stop you because you have the source of all possibilities dwelling in you. Think about it!

ACTION POINT

What are the doubts in your mind that have pegged you to look downward than looking toward Him?

_____

_____

Make it a habit to only think of the way out of every situation, not seeing it as the end.

_____

_____

DAY 26

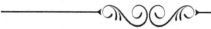

FORMULA FOR GREATER

"My son, give me thine heart, and let thine eyes observe my ways."

Proverbs 23:26 (KJV)

Two keys are needed for you to arrive at your greatness. They are; Surrender and Relationship. You see, all the men in the scripture that came at their greatness were men that first surrendered and then walked with God.

For instance, God told Abraham in Genesis 17:1 (KJV), *"…walk before me, and be thou perfect."* He didn't just leave his Father's house and followed God's instructions, but he also had a pure relationship with God. And in James 2:23, he was called the *friend of God*.

Your heavenly Father wants nothing more than for you to totally surrender your mind, body, and spirit to Him. He desires to have a place of rest in your heart. He doesn't want to come like a visitor who is in today and out the next day. God doesn't want to check-in and out of your life. He wants to dwell in you. He wants your heart and also desires that you seek his ways. Then, He will lead you in the path to your greatness.

Key Success Tip 26:

When you fully surrender peace will follow.

REFLECTION

Abraham, the friend of God, became Abraham the great. What is your stand with God?

ACTION POINT

Have you given it all to God already?

_____

_____

If not, it's time to deliberately list the habits holding you from deeply embracing His love.

_____

_____

Build a relationship with God by renewing your service in His house and His kingdom.

_____

_____

DAY 27

SUBMIT TO GOD'S
PREPARATION PLAN

"And we know that God causes everything to work together for the good of those who love God and are called according to his purpose for them."

Romans 8:28 (NLT)

Corrie Ten Boom once wrote, "Every experience God gives us, every person He puts in our lives is the perfect preparation for the future that only he can see."

Esther submitted to God's preparation plan, and that gave her the ultimate elevation. The elevation wasn't only in her position as the queen but also the happiness in her heart.

God takes time to prepare us for the position we are to fill. Your position may not be a queen's position like Esther. It may be your desire to be a great leader, a business executive, a minister, or a public office holder.

Still, you need to realize that it takes time of preparation for God to place you in such an estimable position.

During the preparation time, you may be tempted to abort the process and take matters into your hands, but it takes little time to know that the way that seems right to many is actually headed for destruction—Proverbs 14:12 (NLT). There is a path before each person that seems right, but it ends in death.

Key Success Tip 27:

Preparation is a recipe for success. Give yourself permission to embrace preparation season.

REFLECTION

Do you acknowledge the Lord's purpose at all? Are you confident in the integrity of God? Don't be impressed with your wisdom. Instead, fear the LORD and depend on him. *"Trust in the LORD with all your heart; do not depend on your own understanding. Seek his will in all you do, and he will direct your paths"* (Proverbs 3:5-6 NLT).

ACTION POINT

In what area you drawing away from God and resisting His discipline for your greatness.

_____

_____

Take every word and experience that God takes you through as preparation for your purpose.

_____

_____

Don't fight it. How will you embrace it?

_____

_____

DAY 28

CAPTURE AND CRYSTALLIZE YOUR IDEAS

"And as Christ's soldier, do not let yourself become tied up in the affairs of this life, for then you cannot satisfy the one who has enlisted you in his army."

2 Timothy 2:4 (NLT)

Do you know what it means to capture and crystallize your ideas? Have you ever take a moment to write them down your ideas? You ask, "Is it necessary to write down what I see?" Absolutely, yes, it is.

Many people have lost sight of where God is taking them to because they fail to write it down. *"And the LORD answered me, and said, write the vision, and make it plain upon tables, that he may run that readeth it"* (Habakkuk 2:2 KJV). And the first thing that the prophet was eager to do was to look out for what the Lord will reveal to him. His preparedness to note the things God will say to him was impeccable.

Your expectations should be high, God being your strength, you wouldn't dwindle, there's the assurance that nothing can snatch you from the Lord's hollow hands! Keep your gaze on him, reflection all He shows to you in humanity.

Take note! The process of writing it down serves as a leap of faith to remind you that the present circumstance remains inferior to the greatness embedded in you. God emphasized this while discussing with Habakkuk. Likewise, you who have read about His plan will be energized to run till it is fulfilled.

Key Success Tip 28:

Place the written vision in a place where you can see it daily.

REFLECTION

Can there be any other plan better than the Lord's? Who knows the beginning from the end? He is Lord today, tomorrow, and forever; depending on him is always profitable. *"For I know the plans I have for you,' says the LORD. 'They are plans for good and not for disaster, to give you a future and a hope"* (Jeremiah 29:11 NLT).

ACTION POINT

Make a list of your ideas no matter how impossible they may seem.

_____

_____

Start taking steps to actualize them.

_____

Unlocking Your Greater

As you conclude this week, what were some of your greatest challenges and successes? And, what are the next steps to continue your forward movement into this upcoming week?

_____
_____
_____
_____
_____
_____
_____
_____
_____
_____
_____
_____
_____
_____
_____
_____
_____
_____

"You Are A Masterpiece"

DAY 29

WALK INTO YOUR GREATER

"The truth is, anyone who believes in me will do the same works I have done, and even greater works, because I am going to be with the Father."

John 14:12 (NLT)

Now is the time to take the steps to greatness. Solomon said, "He that considers the cloud will not sow" (Ecclesiastes 1:40, Trans), so start! Despite adverse prevailing circumstances. The rest of your life is the best of your life.

Start by taking steps of greatness daily, be consistent and never give up; aspire to be better than yesterday's master stroke.

Apostle Paul said, *"I don't mean to say that I have already achieved these things or that I have already reached perfection! But I keep working toward that day when I will finally be all that Christ Jesus saved me for and wants me to be"* (Philippians 3:12 NLT).

Develop yourself daily, subject yourself to continuous improvement. Make greatness your only intent. And you will realize it. It's your time; nothing is a barricade; all your obstacles are surmounted; surely! You must attain your greater height.

Key Success Tip 29:

Celebrate the small victories in your life. It builds momentum.

REFLECTION

Do you think you have reached your greater level? Are you satisfied with your current achievements? Philippians 3:13 (NLT) says, *"No, dear brothers and sisters, I am still not all I should be, but I am focusing all my energies on this one thing: Forgetting the past and looking forward to what lies ahead."*

ACTION PLAN

Those ideas and great plans you had in mind long ago, it's time to actualize them.

_____

_____

Make the needed calls, pray if you have to, read and learn, but ensure that all your steps are targeted to your greatness.

_____

_____

_____

_____

DAY 30

WORDS ARE A SPIRITUAL MYSTERY

"People can tame all kinds of animals and birds and reptiles and fish, but no one can tame the tongue. It is an uncontrollable evil, full of deadly poison."

James 3:7-8 (NLT)

Scripture is filled with principles that support the power of the tongue. Job 22:28, says you will decree a thing, and it will be established. God has deposited so much in you because you were created in His image. He created the world with His words, and He desires you to imitate Him by speaking gracious and edifying words.

Words are a mystery that goes beyond the scope of mere human discernment. They are a divine secret designed to equip you for an unprecedented life of empowerment, influence, and greatness. The Bible reveals that God has given you the ability to speak words that preserve and strengthen.

Colossians 4:6 says, *"Let your speech be always with grace, seasoned with salt, that ye may know how ye ought to answer every man,"* and Isaiah 50:4 says, *"The Lord GOD hath given me the tongue of the learned, that I should know how to speak a word in season to him that is weary…"* In truth, your world is created and sustained by this spiritual material called words.

Therefore, the person who can master and leverage this great power will enter into God's will for them.

If you let the word of God dwell in you, your greatness in his sight will know no bounds!

Key Success Tip 30:

Speak life into your
purpose and surround
yourself with positivity.

REFLECTION

Whose words dwell in you? Do you value the
essence of God's word? What kind of words do you
speak? How do people feel after talking with you?
Your words should edify others and bring glory to
God.

ACTION PLAN

Write down some scriptural quotes and meditate on
them.

_____

_____

_____

_____

DAY 31

GOD IS FOR YOU!

"What shall we say about such wonderful things as these? If God is for us, who can ever be against us?"

Romans 8:31 (NLT)

Presently, the occurrences around the world leave little room for hope. The world appears to be in a great disorder with the COVID-19 pandemic. Through all of these, one thing seems to be startlingly clear: no matter how advanced humanity has become, we are helpless without God.

In truth, there will be trials and tribulations, but what you believe and stand for at this point will determine how great you will become! If you read the text for today further to verse 39, you will see along list of afflictions Paul made, but he ended it by saying, *"...indeed, nothing in all creation will ever be able to separate us from the love of God that is revealed in Christ Jesus our Lord."*

What's your conviction in these difficult times? Are you questioning God, or do you believe Him with all your heart? He has promised never to leave or forsake you.

Key Success Tip 31:

Stand up for your greater today. Maximize your full potential.

REFLECTIONS

Meditate on Psalm 23:4, which says, "even though I walk through the valley of the shadow of death, I will fear no evil, for you are with me, your rod and your staff, they comfort me."

ACTION POINT

How has this current pandemic affected your faith in God?

_____

_____

_____

Write out scriptures that affirm God's presence to you and confess them daily.

_____

_____

_____

_____

DAY 32

SCULPTURED FOR GREATNESS

"Before I formed you in the womb I knew you, before you were born I set you apart; I appointed you as a prophet to the nations."

Jeremiah 1:5 (NIV)

Would you believe me if I said we were all created to be beyond average? The omnipotent God created us in his own image.

Consider your maker; isn't He a great God? What do you expect of His creation? Maybe you've asked yourself the *big* questions: *Why am I here? What am I born to do? Am I even relevant to my world?* Well, the answers lie in your ability to understand and utilize your nature and design. God had a plan in mind when He formed and designed you (Jeremiah 29:11).

So, until you come to a place where you understand the purpose of your existence, you'll continue to struggle with reality. It is unwise to try to fit into what you are not designed for. No one ever achieves greatness in that manner. Imagine square pegs trying to fit in round holes; that would be such an epic fail!

Key Success Tip 32:

Revisit the vision today and see what've you done towards it.

REFLECTION

Your life consists of divinely orchestrated patterns and designs. Discover what you were made to contribute to humanity and invest every bit of your energy to produce your fore ordained greatness.

ACTION POINT

Have you discovered your purpose yet? Yes, or No?

_____

_____

If yes, are you working towards achieving them?

_____

_____

_____

_____

If no, what are the practical steps you are taking to discover them?

_____

_____

_____

DAY 33

SPEAK IT

"From the fruit of their mouth, a person's stomach is filled; with the harvest of their lips, they are satisfied. The tongue has the power of life and death, and those who love it will eat its fruit."

Proverbs 18:20-21(NIV)

Your world is framed by your words, just like God created the world by His words. If you desire greatness, then watch your words.

Have you ever said to yourself, I don't think I'll finish this project, or This Ivy League School is not for people of my racial, financial, or social background? I can't have that job, promotion, profit, house, home, family, and love life? The bible says that our bellies are satisfied with the fruit of our mouth; in other words, we get what we say. If you confess failure, you will have it; and if it is greatness, that's what you will get!

Key Success Tip 33:

Step into your promise by speaking it into existence.

REFLECTION

Your words are powerful; use them wisely. Choose positive speaking over negative confessions. If you speak little of yourself, then you will not achieve greatness. Do yourself a favor; think before you speak.

ACTION POINT

What are those negative words you would like to not say to yourself?

_____

_____

_____

_____

Write down the reverse here and confess them each time you seem vulnerable.

_____

_____

_____

_____

DAY 34

YOUR THOUGHTS ARE A MAGNETIC FIELD

"For as he thinketh in his heart, so is he ..."

Proverbs 23:7 (KJV)

A British philosophical writer, James Allen, wrote, "A man can only rise, conquer, and achieve by lifting his thoughts. He can only remain weak, and abject, and miserable by refusing to lift his thoughts." This shows that life essentially answers to mentality.

In the pursuit of greatness, it is important to note that no man has ever risen beyond his or her mindset. Great men and women think great thoughts, and their thoughts attract greatness to them. What you think shapes your belief system and what you believe ultimately determines your quality of life. To achieve greatness, you must first overcome the worries in your mind.

There is a saying that you are a product of your thoughts. This means that if you think you will fail in an assignment, you start feeling like a failure. And, you will begin to act like a failure until you ultimately fail.

Key Success Tip 34:

Shape your thoughts in love and His plan for your life today.

REFLECTION

You are in your season of greatness, so think and reflect it, and see yourself as great. Don't limit yourself by regarding the impossibilities. Remember, you can do all things through Christ, who strengthens you

(Philippians 4:13). Have excellent thoughts, cultivate a mindset of possibilities, and begin to walk into greatness.

ACTION POINT

What area of your life needs a change of mindset?

_____

_____

_____

What are those thoughts that limit your abilities?

_____

_____

_____

Write out some positive thoughts about yourself.

_____

_____

_____

DAY 35

WIELD THE TWO EDGED SWORD

"For the word of God is quick, and powerful, and sharper than any two-edged sword, piercing even to the dividing asunder of soul and spirit, and of the joints and marrow, and is a discerner of the thoughts and intents of the heart."

Hebrews 4:12 (KJV)

We all grew up acknowledging and approving the notion of people towards us—what we could or couldn't do, who we are, who we are meant to be, and what we'll never become. How many of these things have you allowed to alter your focus and blur yourself-image?

However, these are mere assumptions and opinions; it is only the Word of God concerning you that is true. It will help if you view yourself through the lens of His Word. Dedicate time to the study of the scripture and use it as a weapon to turn your situation around for greatness. God has declared your greatness, and it must come to pass.

Key Success Tip 35:

Remove every negative doubt, fear, or negative confession about yourself.

REFLECTION

Are you afraid of people's assumptions about you? Keep calm, and know what God says concerning your life, then you will know that your greatness is sure!

ACTION POINT

How much time are you willing to dedicate to the study of God's word when hoping for a change?

_____

_____

_____

What are the opinions of others that have held you bound?

_____

_____

_____

What has God said about you? List and confess them daily.

_____

_____

_____

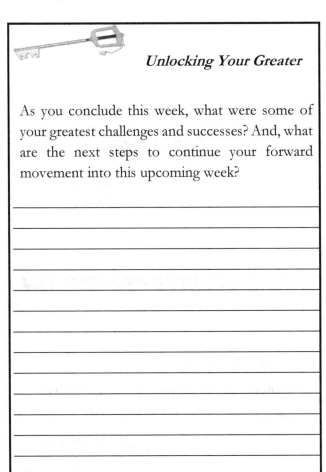

Unlocking Your Greater

As you conclude this week, what were some of your greatest challenges and successes? And, what are the next steps to continue your forward movement into this upcoming week?

"You Are A Masterpiece"

DAY 36

YOU CAN HAVE PERFECTION

"So God created man kind in his own image, in the image of God he created them…"

Genesis 1:27 (NIV)

Today's society makes us feel like we cannot attain perfection. George Orwell once said, "The essence of being human is that one does not seek perfection." However, God's perspective is different from the world's. The Bible says, *"Be ye therefore perfect, even as your Father which is in heaven is perfect"* (Matthew 5:48). God is perfect; thus, as His creation—you can be perfect. The above Bible verse says that God created humankind in his own image. You ought to be like Him. But, until you come into the fullness of His truth, you cannot have this perfection.

Do you think of yourself as "not good enough?" where do you experience imperfection the most? Is it in your character, career, relationship, or walk with God? The Bible records that Job, a man like you, was perfect. God called him a *perfect* and an *upright* man.

Do you know why? It's because his heart was right with God. Perfection starts from the heart. Your heart must, first of all, align with God's heart if you must be as He is. It is also important to note that God doesn't create anything inferior. Genesis1 says, *"And God saw everything that he had made, and, behold, it was very good..."* See yourself through the same lens as God, and you will see perfection.

Key Success Tip 36:

The matters of heart speak and whatsoever you speak takes root.

REFLECTION

You are renewed in the knowledge of God. Don't see yourself as imperfect. You are perfect in Christ, so walk in this consciousness.

ACTION POINT

List the areas of your life where you feel like you can't attain perfection, and say to yourself that you are perfect in Jesus.

_____

_____

_____

DAY 37

PERSISTENCE, DEDICATION, AND FAITH

"Blessed is the man who remains steadfast under trial, for when he has stood the test he will receive the crown of life, which God has promised to those who love him."

James 1:12 (ESV)

Roy T. Bennet said, "The one who falls and gets up is stronger than the one who never tried. Do not fear failure but rather fear not trying." There are traits you must exhibit if you must make giant strides. Here is the story of a man called Derek Anthony. He tore his hamstring at the 1992 Olympic Games in Barcelona as he engaged in the 400 meters semi-finals. Guess what he did afterward? He didn't give up! The story has it that he continued the race, limping, with the assistance of his father. He didn't just continue; he completed a full lap of the track. What courage! You may wonder why he didn't give up. He knew that there was a race he had to finish, irrespective of the challenge he had.

Sometimes, life's circumstances may break you and cause you to question your faith. At such times, you will be faced with the option of either giving up or forging ahead. When you are in this dilemma, choose the latter. It takes a tenacious and a determined mind to fulfill purpose. When your faith is tried, don't be overwhelmed. Trust in God, and depend on his mercy to carry you through. Let me take your mind again to Job. His faith was tested in the course of his walk with God. However, He did not yield to the pressure from the misfortunes that befell him. He was persistent, dedicated to the things of God, and didn't lose hope in God.

Key Success Tip 37:

Challenges arise in our
lives to make us stronger
not defeat us.

REFLECTION

A popular song says, *"Don't give up, it's not over. When you give up, then it's over; hold unto the Lord, your strong and mighty tower…"* When life appears murky and dreary, keep holding the fort.

ACTION POINT

There are Bible characters that experienced failure but didn't give up. Find two of these people, and write down what kept them going.

_____

_____

_____

DAY 38

GRACE- A SPIRITUAL CATALYST

"My grace is sufficient for you, for my power is made perfect in weakness.' Therefore I will boast all the more gladly of my weaknesses, so that the power of Christ may rest upon me."

2 Corinthians 12:9 (KJV)

Greatness is a product of grace. You cannot be outstanding in the kingdom of God except by the grace of our Lord Jesus Christ. God created man to be dependent on Him and not to be self-sufficient. It is expedient to know that you are bound to fail when God is not in what you do.

The truth is that we all have some limitations that can hinder us from achieving greatness, but the grace of God is the catalyst that covers up our inadequacies and amplifies our efforts. With the grace of God, you can access where others may see as inaccessible. It opens doors to possibilities.

Also, God wants you to trust in him with all your heart. When you are dependent on Him, He will direct your path, making rough roads smooth. I want you to know that no matter how difficult your problem is, God's grace is always there to see you through.

Attaining greatness is beyond works. If it is not backed up with grace, then you may crash. Romans 11:6 says, *"but if it is by grace, it is no longer on the basis of works: otherwise, grace would no longer be grace."* Here is a question to ponder: will you keep struggling to get to your greatness, or will you allow God's grace to catapult you to greatness?

Key Success Tip 38:

Accept His grace today,
it is all sufficient.

REFLECTION

Do you feel like you are stuck in your present situation? Does the road to your greatness seem vague? Ask the Lord for His grace, and He will move you beyond the difficult moment.

ACTION POINT

What are those areas of your life that you need divine speed?

_____

_____

_____

DAY 39

TRAIN YOUR SPIRITUAL SENSES

"For, 'who has known the mind of the Lord so as to instruct him?' But we have the mind of Christ."

1 Corinthians 2:16 (NIV)

Man is a triple being; this means that humans are a composite of three distinct components— spirit, soul, and body. These simply mean that as a child of God, you have the Spirit of God in you.

Now, it is important to note that God is Spirit, and he dwells in all believers. You cannot connect with him until your spiritual senses are developed. How? It would be best if you first believed in Him; then yourself to hear in the Spirit. God does not relate with man in the physical realm; everything He does is in the Spirit. So, you must learn to see what He shows you in the spirit realm.

I want you also to know that your greatness has already been purposed spiritually. But, if you must stay on the right track in your journey, the Spirit has to be in control of your life. This can be achieved by having an intimate relationship with Him and constantly feeding on His word.

When you are sensitive in the Spirit, you will flow with what the Holy Spirit is saying or doing. This will help you know what to do at every point in time on your journey to greatness.

Key Success Tip 39:

Training is a prerequisite for success. Remain in a posture of readiness.

REFLECTION

Being sensitive in the Spirit will cause you to grow spiritually and prove that God's word is true. Train your spiritual senses, so you can connect with God and allow Him to guide you.

ACTION POINT

To train your spiritual senses, you must be committed to studying the word and praying. What practical steps will you take towards praying and studying the word of God?

_____

_____

_____

DAY 40

IS THERE A VEIL OF DISGUISE?
(THE 3 TYPES OF MASK)

"Come to me, all you who are weary and burdened, and I will give you rest."

Matthew 11:28 (NIV)

According to a recent developmental study, masking oneself is defined as concealing one's emotion by portraying another emotion. It is mainly used to hide a negative emotion, like sadness, anger, frustration, and more. When there is a part of you that light cannot penetrate, it can hinder you from achieving greatness.

Veils don't reveal the true identity of a person. It gives a false impression of a person, and it can deprive one of beautiful opportunities. However, when you accept who you are and how you feel, you will realize that it will be easier to strive for your greatness.

I will talk about three types of masks. The first is the *unforgiveness mask*. When you don't forgive, your life will be shaped in bitterness, and it could be a roadblock to your greatness. Another type is the *pleasing mask*. This mask makes you always desire to please people, thus, blinding your eyes against the truth. The last one is the *brokenness mask*, which comes with anger, hurt, and more. These veils are exhausting. They drain your courage and enthusiasm for your greatness. But, God is here to help you unmask your true identity.

Key Success Tip 40:

Unmask today so God can use
your full potential in Him.

REFLECTION

Read psalms 34, and ponder it. It is an assurance from God.

ACTION POINT

What are those masks you have been wearing? Write them down, and ask God to take off the masks.

_____

_____

_____

_____

_____

DAY 41

YOU NEED A BETTER REFLECTION

"So all of us who have had that veil removed can see and reflect the glory of the Lord. And the Lord—who is the Spirit—makes us more and more like him as we are changed into his glorious image."

2 Corinthians 3:18 (NLT)

What you see is what you become. In 2 Corinthians 3:8, Paul admonishes us to keep our gaze on God to become like Him. When your attention is on the negativity around you, you will be influenced as well. Everyone deserves a better and brighter reflection, which is found in God.

It's comforting to know that your true greatness is defined in the image of your heavenly Father. Now, it's not about what you set in front of the mirror; it's about the kind of imagery and reflections that you get from it. The Bible says that when you behold God, you will be transformed into God's glorious image, irrespective of who you are.

Key Success Tip 41:

Your mirror reflection looks amazing, believe it!

REFLECTION

What reflection do you have about your life? Are you viewing yourself through a mirror that only diminishes your image of greatness? Do you see yourself less than who you are destined to be? It's high time you make a shift that changes your perception and perspective.

ACTION POINT

What mirror have you been viewing yourself in?

_____

_____

_____

As you view yourself through God's word today, take note of what He says about your greatness.

_____

_____

_____

_____

DAY 42

IMPACT YOUR VISION

"Then the LORD answered me and said, Record the vision and inscribe it on tablets, that the one who reads it may run."

Habakkuk 2:2 (NASB).

Vision is one of the powerful keys to greatness. It is the roadmap to achieving **your greatness**. Your vision must not only be conceptualized in your mind; you must write it as well. There is an active response to move when you see it written down.

And eventually, the vision becomes living when you begin to take active steps to achieve it. Nobody runs well without clarity of vision!

Guess what? You are the first person to believe in your vision! Many times, the eyes that see your glorious destiny are few. However, abandoning your vision for the sake of others is disastrous. You cannot afford to listen to naysayers and those with opposing perspectives. Remember the stories of Noah and Nehemiah in the Bible; imagine what would have happened if they listened to what people said. I am so sure their visions would never have been actualized.

Furthermore, in your pursuit to attain greatness, keeping your head high above the waters of discouragement is paramount. Don't be discouraged, no matter what happens.

Key Success Tip 42:

Remove "stinking thinking" and replace it with a conqueror mindset.

REFLECTION

Write your vision, and run with the resources God has made available to you. Because He is the giver of such vision, He will see to its accomplishment if you keep in step with Him.

ACTION POINT

Write down your vision.

_____

_____

_____

_____

Itemize all you plan to achieve daily and strike them out when they are done.

_____

_____

_____

_____

Unlocking Your Greater

As you conclude this week, what were some of your greatest challenges and successes? And, what are the next steps to continue your forward movement into this upcoming week?

_____

_____

_____

_____

_____

_____

_____

_____

_____

_____

_____

_____

_____

_____

_____

_____

_____

_____

"You Are A Masterpiece"

DAY 43

HAVE A WIN-WIN ATTITUDE

"Now thanks be unto God, which always causeth us to triumph in Christ, and maketh manifest the savor of his knowledge by us in everyplace."

2 Corinthians 2:14 (KJV)

Jeff Keller said: *"Attitude is everything: change your attitude and change your life."* Your outcome in life, whether you will fail or win, starts from the attitude with which you pursue your visions and goals.

I have never seen anyone who talks defeat and ends up a victor. There will be times when it appears your goals and visions are not realistic and worth pursuing. You will be self-defeated, hurt, and ignored by others. However, these are the times when you must demonstrate a high level of faith and grit to see the vision come to pass.

Note that in the text for today, God is seen to *ALWAYS* (not sometimes, not a few times) cause us to triumph. It will be best if you believe this in the face of your biggest failure. Failure is never the end of a child of God. Have an attitude of winning, no matter what, and if you fail, learn from it, and move on.

Key Success Tip 43:

You were built to go the
extra mile so let's win.

REFLECTION

You have to maintain a winning attitude if you want to be great in life. Don't let your past failure define who you are.

ACTION POINT

Write out your past failures and the lessons you have learned from them.

_____

_____

_____

_____

Make a list of scriptural passages that assures you of success at all times, meditate on them and confess them.

_____

_____

_____

_____

DAY 44

TURN YOUR PAIN TO PURPOSE

"Because you know that the testing of your faith produces perseverance."

James 1:3 (NIV)

There will be times in life that you will have to encourage yourself when no one else will. The moments when it seems like you are on a lonely path, and no one understands what you are going through and streams of tears run ceaselessly down your face.

Greatness, on its path, is laced with the pain of discouragement. And this is the defining moment for everyone. The purpose of your trials is not to make you fall on the wayside but to bring out the best in you. These times are difficult; the only way to sustain your vision is to look up to God for strength.

Rather than allow your moment of pain to cause a setback, consider the purpose of the pain as away to bring your attention back to your source, which is God.

Key Success Tip 44:

Your pain is a setup for your comeback. You were created to thrive.

REFLECTION

Every pain has a purpose; seek to know the purpose of yours. Meditate on James 1: 2-4 and see how God orchestrates your journey through the hard times. Life is a marathon, not as print; let the pain of your race propel you to the finishing line.

ACTION POINT

Make a list of your current and past pain.

_____

_____

_____

_____

Ask God to open your eyes to see why you have to go through them. Write them down.

_____

_____

_____

_____

DAY 45

PLUG INTO GOD'S LOVE

"For God so loved the world that he gave his one and only Son, that whoever believes in him shall not perish but have eternal life."

John 3:16 (NIV)

God's love for humanity is an undebatable truth. Whether you will experience it or not, depends solely on you. God desires that you move from a neutral relationship with Him and fully embrace his love and glory.

Jenny B. Jones In her book, *There You'll Find Me*, asks, *"Does your love reach this far, God? And if it extends to heaven and beyond … why can't it seem to find me?"* I have a simple answer to these questions: because you're not plugged in! That's why the love of God seems like a fairytale to you.

God's love is ever-present and available. You don't need to search for it, and you don't have to give anything to obtain it. God gave his only begotten son to save you. He didn't demand anything from you to sacrifice His only son. So, plug into His love today.

Key Success Tip 45:

Experience His love today
by letting go of the past.

REFLECTION

The degree to which you experience God's love is the degree to which you plugin. God will not withhold His love from us. You cannot truly be great without experiencing God's love.

ACTION POINT

Do you believe in God's love?

_____

_____

_____

DAY 46

SUCCESS IS BUILT ON FOUNDATION

"Though the rain comes in torrents and the floodwaters rise and the winds beat against that house, it won't collapse, because it is built on rock."

Matthew 7:25 (NLT)

Have you ever seen a building without foundations? No matter how stunning such edifice appears, it is unsafe for anyone who dares to live in it. Similarly, while trying to attain your greatness, you can consider any success achieved without due process, time, effort, and consistency as a foundationless success. It simply means such success was not fought for, so, it will be short-lived.

To achieve your greatness, you must be deeply rooted like the high Chinese bamboo tree. You must be patient and persistent en route to your dream. Be determined; learn to disregard failure and surmount obstacles, endure the challenges that come your way. This process makes you deep-rooted and creates a strong foundation upon which success can be sustained.

Spiritually, you must willingly follow the Lord's gentle steps in making you matured; it's not going to happen overnight. That's why you should be transformed daily, according to Romans 12:2.

You may want greater achievements, greater happiness, and greater fulfillment. But you should understand that such desired success and greatness is a product of persistence. Of course, nothing reliable can be built without a good foundation.

Key Success Tip 46:

Success is created and
sustained based upon
the foundation you lay.

REFLECTION

Do you know the extent of your desired success and
its required foundation? Will, you rather cut corners
than make a reliable track record for your desired
greatness? "When the rains and floods come and the
winds beat against that house, it will fall with a
mighty crash" Mathew 7:27 (NLT.)

ACTION POINT

What foundations are you determined to build in
preparation for your future success?

_____

_____

_____

DAY 47

THINK SYSTEMATICALLY

"And now, dear brothers and sisters, let me say one more thing as I close this letter. Fix your thoughts on what is true and honorable and right. Think about things that are pure and lovely and admirable. Think about things that are excellent and worthy of praise."

Philippians 4:8 (NLT)

Can a great person who has not pondered on how to serve the Lord and humanity arrive at a non-selfish thought? No thoughts from such a heart can be satisfactory before God.

In seeking God, there are no limitations, no shortage of thought or ideas. Henceforth, make a habit of seeking God, develop a relationship with him, be influenced by his thoughts, take the limits off your mind.

God is willing to give you unlimited ideas, don't limit yourself, gear up! Be decisive at heart; let your thoughts be unrestricted. Think about how to be impactful towards humanity; God wants you to think in a systematically approved way.

Make declarations; "I agree with God that greatness is mine, God has destined me to bear great fruits to serve humanity, my thoughts must not limit me, I will put efforts to achieve greatness."

With God's help, you have all it takes to reach the peak. Your greatness is now!

Key Success Tip 47:

Be intentional in your pursuit for purpose. Let nothing get in your way.

REFLECTION

Are you light-hearted concerning your future? Do you feel hopeless? Awaken the giant within you! Do you have a relationship with God? He is a well of limitless ideas, seek God today, and possess wealth of ideas.

ACTION POINT

What areas have you been selfish? Decide to be selfless today, and boldly execute your thoughts.

_____

_____

_____

DAY 48

HONE YOUR SKILLS

"Do you see a man skillful in his work? He will stand before kings; he will not stand before obscure men."

Proverbs 22:29 (ESV)

God is the giver of good and perfect gift. Yet, he expects us to maintain such gifts and use them to serve humanity.

If you want to be great, you must maintain a close relationship with God; your pursuits should be divinely ordered. David was a shepherd; he fought wild animals to protect his flock, he delivered his lamb from the jaws of a lion. He gained battle skills as a shepherd and risked his life many times. These experiences made his roots deep as he grew greater and stronger.

Do not despise your gift; instead, enhance it by the opportunities you get—be consistent. Your capacity will improve if laziness is not allowed. The older a wine gets, the sweeter; you'll improve your skill by perpetual training. Don't be discouraged; little drops of water make a mighty ocean. God operates progressively over His creations; God's model for **your greatness** is to grow from strength to strength; He is a master at improving all things' worth. Shouldn't His gift in you grow exponentially too?

Key Success Tip 48:

Redefine or define your why? This will help you develop your skills for success.

REFLECTION

Have you harnessed the gifts in you for the benefit of humanity? Are you satisfied with your minimal performance, or you're ready to hone your skills and achieve greatness?

ACTION POINT

Identify skills and talents in your life that need refining.

_____

_____

_____

Write down practical ways you intend to hone your skills.

_____

_____

_____

Unlocking Your Greater

As you conclude this week, what were some of your greatest challenges and successes? And, what are the next steps to continue your forward movement into this upcoming week?

"You Are A Masterpiece"

DAY 49

ALIGN FOR GREATER MANIFESTATION

"The future glory of this Temple will be greater than its past glory, says the LORD Almighty.

And in this place I will bring peace. I, the LORD Almighty, have spoken!"

Haggai 2:9 (NLT)

Imagine you got distracted and wrongly placed a bucket of water before a rushing tap of water, you will agree with me that your time and resources have been wasted. This is the scenario when you fail to align for the manifestation of greatness; regardless of preparations, if you aren't properly aligned, greatness may elude you. Preparations should be aligned towards manifestation.

God prepared David; he wrestled with wild animals while protecting the flock. His manifestation was in the great victory against Goliath. God specifically prepared him while he was a shepherd; warding off several wild animals, he even killed some. God aligned and prepared David in a specific way for his greater manifestation.

Is God sharpening you, or you've declared independence from God? "Not by strength, nor by power, but by my spirit says the Lord." Without God in the mix as the origin of any greatness, such greatness is of temporal value.

Do you want to prepare in vain? If not, you should cling to God and submit to his preparation plan. Your journey to greatness depends on how much your roots grow in God; God is the master planner; he will align you for a greater manifestation.

Key Success Tip 49:

Prepare to walk in purpose by filling your cup with a mindset of, "I can" and "I will".

REFLECTION

Do you want a greater manifestation? Are you ready to align with God for greatness?

ACTION POINT

Alignment takes deliberate effort! What intentional steps are you taking towards alignment?

_____

_____

_____

What are those things in your life that need alignment the most?

_____

_____

DAY 50

CELEBRATE THE SMALL WINS

"And people should eat and drink and enjoy the fruits of their labor, for these are gifts from God."

Ecclesiastes 3:13 (NLT)

The Israelites, on their way to the Promised Land, murmured and repeatedly grumbled against Moses. This was after they escaped from slavery in Egypt, and they saw Pharaoh's army perish in the red sea.

They were not grateful to God for the deliverance. Instead, they rebelled against God and compelled Aaron into molding an idol in the absence of Moses. They were rebellious and focused on their several inadequacies in the wilderness. At a point, Instead of focusing on God's many mercies and grace, they were ready to go back to slavery in Egypt.

They didn't celebrate nor appreciate the victory from slavery; they felt the Promised Land journey was long. Because of their murmurings, many of them perished and never made it to the Promised Land.

Celebrate small victories because they lead to your greatness. Don't be discouraged, Keep pressing; difficult times will come, but you must be persistent towards greatness. Remind yourself of God's little mercies, don't lose faith in your desired greatness.

Every plant experienced growth before yielding fruits. Except a grain of wheat is planted, it remains the same. You may be at the seed level for now, but don't lose sight of the potential in you. Be thankful that you are a viable seed. Cherish your growth!

Key Success Tip 50:

Remain diligent in your pursuit of purpose and celebrate a victory today.

REFLECTION

Do you keep a record of God's faithfulness to you? Are you grumbling against God? To achieve greatness, you need to be brave and positive-minded while you celebrate the small victories!

ACTION POINT

Write down moments in which you were ungrateful and repent of ingratitude.

_____

_____

_____

What areas of your life are you particularly grateful for? Learn to focus on them!

_____

_____

_____

DAY 51

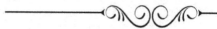

TAKE ACTIONABLE STEPS TO YOUR GREATNESS

"Lazy people want much but get little, but those who work hard will prosper and be satisfied."

Proverbs 13:4 (NLT)

Among many hindrances to your greatness are; pride, laziness, and cowardice. Prayer is the first actionable step to all these hindrances. The Lord promised to change our hearts of stone to hearts of flesh.

If you are proud, beware that God resists the proud but gives grace to the humble. You should work towards humility, and be conscious of the position of your heart; always present yourself to God in prayer. Pride goes before a fall; this means that pride is capable of making you forfeit greatness if at all you achieved it.

It takes effort and a tough mentality to achieve great heights today. Anyone with a fragile heart must become courageous if they must attain the height of greatness. Bold and progressive steps are essential in your quest for greatness.

You can't maintain a couch potato's position, waiting for things to happen at their pace. Smell the coffee! Take actionable steps, pay the price; you're entitled to greatness!

Key Success Tip 51:

Each step taken toward your purpose is an active step toward fulfilling your destiny.

REFLECTION

Do you want greatness by taking actionable steps henceforth? Will you assess the areas that may hinder your journey to success and work on them?

ACTION POINT

Define your greatness by writing down your long term goals.

_____

_____

What actionable steps are you taking towards your greatness?

_____

_____

_____

_____

DAY 52

LIFT YOUR THOUGHTS

"Don't copy the behavior and customs of this world, but let God transform you into a new person by changing the way you think. Then you will know what God wants you to do, and you will know how good and pleasing and perfect his will really is."

Romans 12.2 (NLT)

Why should you be downcast? Why should you be distressed? Your current phase of life might be as a result of your poor relationship with God. Once your relationship is mended, your thoughts will be lifted.

Your situation may be devastating; the burden of not accomplishing your expectations in due time may be discouraging. Tears roll down your cheek as you reflect on missing the mark; your passion dwindles, then depression sets in.

"How did I end here" you wonder! You realize that a big part of your sad condition is due to self-doubt, and the judgments of naysayers stuck in your head. It's high time you break free from the shackles of these influences; through Christ, cling to your unlimited potentials, your thoughts will be lifted.

Don't be *boxed in* if you want greatness; think freely, keep high hopes. Don't be limited to the unproductive status quo in the world, rather, be transformed by the altitudes of possibilities in God's refreshing words. Just as Wayne Dyer puts it, "The only limits you have are the limits you believe."

When life knocks you down, get up! Try again, defy the odds, and lift your thoughts beyond the barriers of deterring occurrences.

Key Success Tip 52:

There are many ways to achieve purpose. Choose one and stick with it.

REFLECTION

What areas of your life need lifting? Do you reckon God's capability of refreshing you? Will you be invigorated?

ACTION POINT

Gear up! Determine not to remain on the ground, be inspired, and let God refresh you!

DAY 53

PUSH THE RE-SET BUTTON

"Zeal without knowledge is not good; a person who moves too quickly may go the wrong way."

Proverbs 19:2 (NLT)

One of the rules in sprint game is that each athlete must maintain their lane till the finishing line. Any athlete who doesn't keep to this will be disqualified. Unfortunately, this is the pattern many seem to follow in life; they started on the wrong foot; if they keep at it, failure is inevitable. This is when there-set button should be pressed.

God must sanction your adventure towards greatness. It's high time you inquire of him about your purpose in life before you embark on any kind of pursuits. *"For I know the plans that I have you declares the LORD, plans to prosper you with a future and a hope"* Jeremiah 29:11(KJV). Christ has intentional plans for your greatness.

If you notice that your present pursuit contrasts God's leading in you, push the reset button, begin anew, and align with his leading. It's better late than never; the death and resurrection of Christ are symbolic of a re-set button pressed on behalf of humanity, so that man's purpose may be realigned for true greatness.

Don't complicate matters by over thinking your situation, avoid a dead-end, re-set your goals; it's never too late! Greatness is unlimited, and it's for the persistent.

Key Success Tip 53:

Do not over analyze the road to purpose. Hit the reset button if you get distracted. It's never too late to begin again.

REFLECTION

Are you still on track? Are you still in alignment with God's purpose for you? Greatness is for the purposeful!

ACTION POINT

What areas of your life do you need to press the reset button?

_____

_____

_____

DAY 54

NO LIMITS AND BOUNDARIES

"So don't get tired of doing what is good. Don't get discouraged and give up, for we will reap a harvest of blessing at the appropriate time."

Galatians 6:9 (NLT)

The journey to greatness may seem long and require painstaking efforts. You must not allow its demands to shut your spirit out; you must keep dreaming big, envisioning greatness from your mind. Don't grow weary; at most, take a deep breath, and cool off, but don't give up!

Persevere beyond the limitations, break the boundaries.

There's no limit to your heights if you're passionate about serving God and humanity. Yes, the going may get tough, but be tough enough to press on! Don't entertain defeating thoughts from anyone; not your spouse, your colleague, not even family, don't be limited by their short-sightedness towards greatness. Keep up with their requirements; keep hitting the spot.

Avoid excuses; be bold to take the giant stride towards breakthrough. Be unfettered from the shackles that seem to hold you; Jim Carrey once said, "Maybe other people will try to limit me, but I don't limit myself."

Many who were confronted with several limitations broke through; they defied the odds. Nothing should hinder your quest for greatness; emulate their guts; being in Christ affords you the chances of a limitless breakthrough; take advantage today!

Key Success Tip 54:

Keep pushing toward the goal. Rely on your inner strength and will to reach purpose in your life.

REFLECTION

Are you deceived to be limited? Do you want to experience the limitless heights in Christ? Don't be caught dead with complacency; break the limits!

ACTION POINT

Make a resolution to leverage the limitless opportunities in Christ!

_____

_____

_____

_____

DAY 55

FIGHT TO WIN

"Use every piece of God's armor to resist the enemy in the time of evil, so that after the battle you will still be standing firm."

Ephesians 6:13 (NLT)

In 1 Corinthians 9: 27, Famous Apostle Paul discussed how he carefully fought many issues while preaching the gospel. He emulated a boxer who hardened his body with blows before throwing calculated punches at his opponent. He doesn't beat the air and emerges

victorious in every battle. You must also fight to win!
Victory is your target, and you must not fight for fun,
be vigilant.

In your quest for greatness, be prepared to defend
your goals. You must be willing to fight for success.
Daily targets and plans must be met; if you struggled
to meet up, it's time to break free. Do the essential
things, especially when you don't feel like; be
consistent, it's a real fight, and victory is the only goal.

Conflicting thoughts may ensue, be decisive; your
purpose is worth fighting for, give it a shot. Don't be
discouraged, don't be tired; be invigorated, be your
number one fan! Inspire yourself; coast to victory!
Throwing in the towel is not an option. Victory will
be yours at last.

Key Success Tip 55:

Do not let your guard down
remain steadfast and unmovable
today. You are almost there!

REFLECTION

Do you feel your strength is sapped? Do you feel burdened? Never give up? Give it a shot!

ACTION POINT

Write down the ways in which you will defend your goals.

_____

_____

_____

How are you going to ensure consistency in meeting your daily targets and goals?

_____

_____

_____

_____

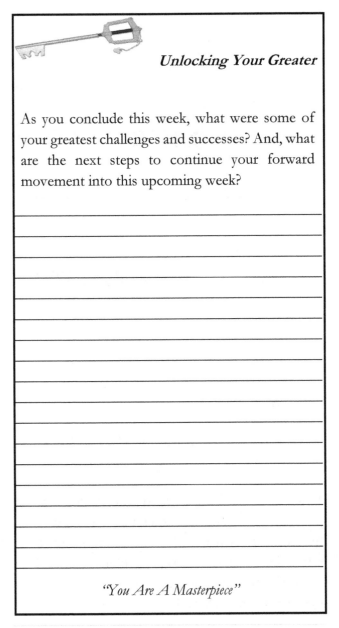

Unlocking Your Greater

As you conclude this week, what were some of your greatest challenges and successes? And, what are the next steps to continue your forward movement into this upcoming week?

_____
_____
_____
_____
_____
_____
_____
_____
_____
_____
_____
_____
_____
_____
_____
_____
_____
_____

"You Are A Masterpiece"

DAY 56

YOUR TONGUE LEGISLATES

"Death and life are in the power of the tongue, and those who love it will eat its fruit."

Proverbs 18:21 (NKJV)

Your mouth is the gateway to your realities. What you say and think about end up molding your realities in life, whether good or otherwise. It's been established that the power of intention, which is expressed through the thoughts in our minds and the words we speak, will eventually affect all things that matter to us. This goes to show that what you think and say will determine the trajectory of your life.

What do you say when faced with hurdles on the track of greatness? What is your confession when you are faced with challenges? What do you pronounce into your destiny? Your words have no geographical limitations. When they are released, they're suspended and incubated until the time for its manifestation comes forth.

For instance, the children of Israel wandered in the wilderness not because they lacked direction but because they legislated their wandering exile with their negative and ungrateful chatter (Numbers14:1-10).

Key Success Tip 56:

Encourage yourself today, you are one step closer to purpose.

REFLECTION

Your words are powerful and have prophetic insinuation. Just as building experts take raw materials to construct timeless monuments, your words are raw materials that can take you to your greatness. Be intentional in choosing the right words always.

ACTION POINT

What are you confessing into your life?

_____

_____

What are your words of greatness?

_____

_____

_____

DAY 57

WHERE ARE YOU PLANTED?

"And he shall be like a tree planted by the rivers of water, that bringeth forth his fruit in his season; his leaf also shall not wither; and whatsoever he doeth shall prosper."

Psalm 1:3 (KJV)

Jesus told a parable about a sower who went out to sow. Some of the seeds fell along the path; some fell on rocky places; others fell among thorns. They grew up but couldn't stay long because the thorns choked them. Still, other seeds fell on good soil, where they produced crops—a hundred, sixty, or thirty times what was sown.

The problem is not with these environmental impediments—rock, thorns—which prevent the seeds from blossoming. Every seed that has life surely has the potential of becoming a fruitful tree. For an apple seed, it has apples in it. For a rose bush, it has blossoms in it.

Just like the seed, you are full of talents, gifts, and potential, which can only thrive in the right kind of environment. Hanging around negative people who have no goal, motivation and are narrow-minded will impede your progress to your greatness because your place of planting is your place of dominance and prominence.

This will help you overcome all distractions as you advance to your greatness. Do not allow any hindrance to distract you from moving into your greatness. You are worth it, and God is ready and willing to walk alongside you as you run full speed ahead to your greatness.

> ## Key Success Tip 57:
>
> Settle your mind and thoughts today as move you move into purpose.

REFLECTION

Check your sphere of influence on your journey to your greatness; are there friends who waste your time and energy? You have to be selective about this. The truth is, *"You're the average of the five people you spend the most time with."*—Jim Rohn.

ACTION POINT

Where are you planted?

_____

_____

_____

Where has God positioned you?

_____

_____

DAY 58

CHART UNKNOWN
TERRITORIES

"...The LORD said to Abram, "Look as far as you can see in every direction— north and south, east and west. I am giving all this land, as far as you can see, to you and your descendants as a permanent possession..."

Genesis 13:14-17 (NLT)

Your feet will never take you to where your mind has not been. For you to conquer new territories, you must have the courage to lose sight of any likely storm as you head for the shore.

Christopher Columbus was an Italian explorer who dared to lose sight of the known to experience the unknown. It was confirmed that his *journey marked the beginning of centuries of transatlantic colonization. But this could only have happened because he dared to chart unknown territories.*

Learn to dream big and wake up each day to fulfill every task and assignment required to experience your greatness. Unleash the power you've got on your mind and cultivate possibility thinking. God told Abraham, "I will give this land to you and your seed forever as far as his eyes can see." God is saying to you, too, as far as your eyes can see, you will walk into your greatness.

Key Success Tip 58:

The journey to purpose is not a sprint but a marathon. Enjoy the ride!

REFLECTION

Allow God to download into your mind cutting-edge tactics and strategies that will propel you to your greatness.

ACTION POINT

As God reveals the secrets, write them down, and take steps to achieve them. Go confidently in the direction of your greatness.

_____

_____

_____

DAY 59

TRUST GOD'S OUTCOME

"For my thoughts are not your thoughts, neither are your ways my ways," declares the LORD."

Isaiah 55:8 (NIV)

As you journey to your greatness, you'll need to stay anchored to God in all situations. For instance, nobody sits on a seat without first trusting that the chair is capable of bearing their weight. The truth is, hardship will either propel you to move forward into **your greatness** or peg you down to accept your fate hopelessly. The pebbles that life throws at you can either be used to build a wall that keeps you from moving forward or a bridge to crossover all impossibilities to your greatness. Therefore, you must be willing to choose at the onset of any hardship either to trust God completely, or you stop pursuing a life of impact.

God wants you to be like Jesus in the fishing boat, asleep, that is, in the midst of crisis and storm. While others are disturbed, express your boldness in God by staying seated. Take a nap, and rest assured that your anchor is not made of metal and rope that some kind of storm can break. Jehovah, the strongest of all, is your anchor.

Key Success Tip 59:

Remain in relationship with Christ as he molds and shapes purpose in your life.

REFLECTION

Do you trust God's outcome even at moments when you don't seem to understand what is happening?

Do you believe that God makes everything beautiful in His own time? (Ecclesiastes 3:11)

ACTION POINT

Starting now, commit to seeking God like never before; write down ways you're going to develop a deeper connection with Him.

_____

_____

_____

DAY 60

MAKE JOURNALS FOR YOUR JOURNEY

"For the vision is yet for an appointed time; But at the end it will speak, and it will not lie.

Though it tarries, wait for it; Because it will surely come, It will not tarry."

Habakkuk 2:3 (NKJV)

More than a thousand fleeting thoughts, a written word can light up the fire in our hearts. Writings or journals remind you of where you are going and prevent you from settling where you are? We all need a form of compass in our hands that guides our minds as we navigate the path to greatness. If you want to make any decision and you need something to aid your thought or focus, and guidance for decisions, then write down your vision and make it plain. You have a responsibility to keep yourself on track to your glorious destination. Don't neglect it!

You see, the process of writing it down leads us to take a running leap of faith to believe that we are much greater than our current circumstance. God emphasized this while discussing with Habakkuk. God says that anyone who reads about His greatness plan for them would be energized to run until it is fulfilled.

Key Success Tip 60:

Day 60, run the race He has given you and in the end you will reap every perfect gift from above on earth.

REFLECTION

Plainly written visions and goals help us to fix our gaze on the greatness that lies ahead of us in the face of apparent impossibilities. Hence, there is a need for you to write down what God is showing you.

ACTION POINT

What has God spoken to you about in recent days? What steps have you taken toward achieving them?

Where have you failed in obeying God? What instructions are you determined to carry out? Ask the Holy Spirit to help you.

ABOUT
KHARIS PUBLISHING

KHARIS PUBLISHING is an independent, traditional publishing house with a core mission to publishimpactful books, and channel proceeds into establishing mini-libraries or resource centers for orphanages in developing countries, so these kids will learn to read, dream, and grow. Every time you purchase a book from Kharis Publishing or partner as an author, you are helping give these kids an amazing opportunity to read, dream, and grow. Kharis Publishing is an imprint of Kharis Media LLC. Learn more at
https://www.kharispublishing.com.